GROWING CHILLIES

A Guide to the Domestic Cultivation of Chilli Plants

JASON NICKELS

Growing Chillies

A Guide to the Domestic Cultivation of Chilli Plants

Author: Jason Nickels

Published by: Jason Nickels

ISBN: 978-0-9574446-0-7

First Edition, 2012

Published in the United Kingdom

Designed by Chandler Book Design
www.chandlerbookdesign.co.uk

TABLE OF CONTENTS

CHAPTER ONE

Introduction 3

The Environment and the Use of Peat 4

CHAPTER TWO

About Chillies 7

Origins 7

Chilli Heat: the Scoville Scale 7

Capsaicin 7

Heat Measurement 7

Chilli Species and Varieties 8

CHAPTER THREE

Growing Conditions 13

Can I grow chillies where I live? 13

Is my house or garden suitable? 14

Temperatures 14

Light 14

What about a greenhouse? 15

Glass Greenhouses 15

Polytunnels 16

Plastic Greenhouses and Covered Shelves 16

Self-Watering Systems 16

Hydroponics and Artificial Light 17

CHAPTER FOUR

Choosing What to Grow 23

Variety Names 24

Planning your Year 25

Suggested Varieties 26

CHAPTER FIVE

Sowing Seeds 33

What Essentials do I Need? 33
Soil 33
Pots 34
Propagators 35
When to Sow 36
How Many to Sow 36
How to Sow 37
Warmth 37
Watering 37
Germination 38
Airflow 39
Oops! Nothing has happened 39
Growing Kits 39

CHAPTER SIX

Caring for Seedlings 43

Pots and Soil 43
Transplanting 44
Light 44
Feeding 45
Watering 45
Spraying or Watering in Sunlight 45
Oops! They all seem to be dying 46
Damping-Off 46
Sun Damage and Hardening-Off 47

CHAPTER SEVEN

Larger Plants 51

What Essentials do I Need? 51
Pots and Soil 51
Growing in the Ground 53
Light.... again 54
Feeding 54
Why is some plant feed better than others? 55
Fed and Unfed Plants 55
Pruning 56
Flowers 57
Pollination 57
Flower-Drop 58

Fruit Development 59
Capsaicin Levels: Can I make my chillies hotter? 60
Colour and Heat 60
What is Normal and What Isn't? 61
My chillies are going black! 61
Variegated Plants 62
Corking 62
Harvest Time 63
When to Pick 63
How to Pick 63
Don't Delay Picking 63

CHAPTER EIGHT

Pests, Diseases and Other Problems 67
Me! 67
Biological Control of Pests 67
Companion Planting 68
Overwatering 68
Slugs and Snails 69
Greenfly and Blackfly (Aphids) 71
Whitefly 73
Caterpillars and Grubs 73
Red Spider Mite 74
Fungus Gnats 75
Viral, Bacterial and Fungal Infections 76
Bacterial Spot 76
Blossom-End Rot 76
Verticillium Wilt 77
Tobacco Mosaic Virus 77
Phytophthora Blight 77
Sunscald 77
Mice 78

CHAPTER NINE

Keeping Plants Over Winter 81
Some Varieties are Better than Others 81
Temperature 81
Feed and Water 82
Re-potting 82
Pruning 82
Removing Fruit 82

CHAPTER TEN

What to do with Your Chilli Crop 85
- Freezing 85
- Drying 86
- Smoking 87
- Pickling 88
- Chilli Oil 88
- Hot Sauce 89

CHAPTER ELEVEN

What's Next? 93
- More Difficult Varieties 93
- Harvesting and Keeping Seeds 94
- Breeding and Cross-Pollination 94

Resources 99

Index 101

Acknowledgments 105

About the Author 105

INTRODUCTION

CHAPTER ONE
Introduction

This book is written for growers in the UK, Northern Europe and the temperate regions of North America in mind. However, a chilli is a chilli and the same principles apply wherever you are in the world.
You know, better than anybody, what your local climate is like and, when reading this book, you will soon get to know what factors you need to think about when deciding on how to care for your plants.
For example, southern hemisphere readers will need to translate any mention of south facing windows as of course you will look north to see the sunshine. You will also need to reverse the seasons so where March to September applies in the UK, in New Zealand, for example, you will be thinking of September to March.

My approach is a practical one and addresses the common questions and problems I know the novice or average chilli grower will face. I hope not to baffle you with science too much, but sometimes a little extra knowledge helps with understanding how or why things happen the way they do.

A short word about spelling; being British I have chosen to use 'chilli' which is generally the accepted spelling in the UK. In the USA 'chile' is the common spelling for the fruit and 'chili' with a single 'L' for a cooked dish of 'chiles'. Confusing for some, but there is no right or wrong so use whatever is comfortable for you.

At the end of the book there is a resources section to help with the sourcing of seeds and other commercial products that the chilli grower might need.

The Environment and the Use of Peat

Throughout the book I tend to recommend a John Innes compost equivalent. John Innes is a tried and tested recipe formulated decades ago by the John Innes Institute and traditionally includes peat as an ingredient. For those that don't know, peat, much like oil and gas, is an unsustainable resource and harvesting it has a devastating environmental impact. Peat bogs are a disappearing natural habitat, and one which suffers almost exclusively because of the demands of the domestic gardener. The extraction of peat also releases huge amounts of carbon dioxide into the atmosphere. Various compost manufacturers are members of the John Innes Institute and make the 'recipe' under licence as the successful formula has become a favourite amongst gardeners who regard the name as synonymous with quality and are reluctant to risk an alternative. There are now a number of good quality manufacturers of peat-free soil-based John Innes type composts, many large organisations such as the Royal Horticultural Society and the National Trust have already made the move to peat-free composts and we should all do the same. Chilli plants are actually not that fussy, although they do enjoy soil-based compost which has an added advantage of keeping a large plant more stable through the extra weight of loam and sand. If you can't find a peat-free John Innes equivalent at your local garden centre then have a look online, the companies that supply it can put you in touch with a stockist or sometimes supply direct. There is a recommendation at the end of this book.

ABOUT CHILLIES

CHAPTER TWO

About Chillies

Origins

All chillies, wherever you find them in the world, originate from South or Central America. Archaeological evidence from South America has proved their use in cooking at least 4,000 years ago. The first Spanish and Portuguese settlers took them, along with potatoes and tobacco, to other parts of the globe where the ability of chillies to cross-breed resulted in those places developing their own distinct varieties and adapting their cuisine to accommodate them. Today, the chilli in its various forms, is one of the most widely distributed food plants.

Chilli Heat: the Scoville Scale

Capsaicin

Capsaicin is the chemical contained in chillies which causes us pain when we eat it. It is the main representative of a group of capsaicinoid chemicals present to a greater or lesser degree in chillies. They cause a sensation of pain by stimulating those nerves which detect heat. Exposure to the levels of capsaicin found in chillies does not result in actual physiological damage, just the feeling of discomfort. Industrially extracted capsaicin, in its pure form, can be very dangerous though. Everything in moderation!

Heat Measurement

The heat in chillies is traditionally illustrated using the Scoville Scale. This was a measurement invented by a scientist named Wilbur Scoville in 1912 and used a panel of human tasters who were asked to sip increasingly concentrated solutions of diluted chilli extract up to the point where the heat could be detected. If the solution was detectable when the chilli was diluted 200,000 times then this would be translated to 200,000 Scoville Heat Units (SHU). Nowadays the concentration is measured using a process called liquid chromatography, a technical and much more accurate process.

Chilli Species and Varieties

There are 5 common species of chilli, and within these 5 species there are over 3,000 varieties. These varieties have evolved or have been bred over time, either by accident or design, to suit certain climatic conditions, culinary uses, disease resistance or commercial need. This chapter is an overview of the species and their characteristics. For a more detailed selection of different varieties and their uses see the chapter on choosing what to grow.

These are the 5 main chilli species

Capsicum frutescens

(which includes Tabasco, smaller Thai, Birdseye, African Bird and Brazilian Malagueta)

Thai Sun – Capsicum frutescens

These are mostly tall but tight bushes with small fiery hot fruits ranging from 50,000 to 100,000 SHU. Some varieties are slower growing and given to a perennial habit in the right conditions. Tabasco chillies, used in the famous sauce, are grown over a period of three years and their crop is greatest in the second year. Many *Capsicum frutescens* show more of a dislike to low light levels than other species. Even in a bright location, but sheltered from direct sunlight they will grow straggly with long inter-nodal (between the dividing stems) lengths. In strong, direct sunlight, they will produce a much more compact bushy plant.

Capsicum chinense

(which includes Habañero and Scotch Bonnet)

These are generally characterised by broad leaves, a spreading plant habit and a hot chilli with a distinctive, fruity flavour and aroma. They are most often associated with Caribbean cuisine but there are also varieties found in Africa and Asia. The fruit are generally very hot, ranging from 100,000 to over 1 million SHU.

Chichen Itza – Capsicum chinense

Capsicum annuum

(which includes Sweet Peppers, Jalapeño, Cayenne, Pimento, Wax Chillies and many others)

These are taller plants, generally quicker fruiting and vary in heat from nothing at all to around 80,000 SHU. They are the most widespread chilli species. The red and green peppers you might buy in your supermarket are *Capsicum annuum*, just a genetic variation from smaller, hotter varieties.

Jalapeño – Capsicum annuum

Capsicum baccatum

(which includes South American Aji)

Usually a smaller leaved, strong stemmed but bushy shrub. Generally these are smaller, hotter fruits and the plants are more tolerant to cooler climates, bright sunshine and dry conditions. Heat levels range from 3,000 to 100,000 SHU.

Aji – Capsicum baccatum

Capsicum pubescens

(which includes South American Rocoto)

Larger plants with hairy leaves and stems, the fruit often has black seeds. They are said to have a very distinctive heat that quickly overpowers. Some varieties can grow 5 feet tall and 5 feet across so if you grow these make sure you know what you are letting yourself in for. These are generally hot varieties, reaching up to 100,000 SHU.

Rocoto – Capsicum pubescens

Within each species there are many varieties, much like potatoes, tomatoes or roses, and these varieties will cross-pollinate easily and sometimes across species too. This is a double-edged sword, it makes creating new varieties relatively easy but saving seed is a problem as the seed you keep may not be true to its parent plant. See the section on breeding and cross-pollination for more details.

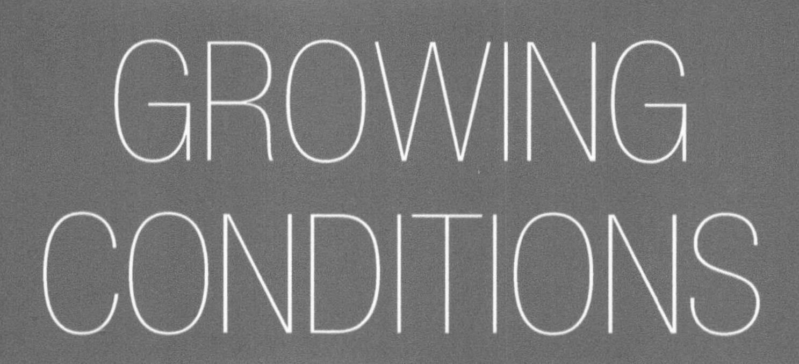

GROWING CONDITIONS

CHAPTER THREE

Growing Conditions

Firstly, let's consider where chilli plants come from and therefore what conditions they are likely to need in order to thrive.

Some, such as *Capsicum chinense* (for example Habañero or Scotch Bonnet) originate from more tropical jungle conditions, the plants don't grow too tall and the stems spread wide. These are suited to more humid conditions and are more tolerant of shade.

Others, such as some of the *Capsicum baccatum* originate from the more open and hostile Andean mountains, and they enjoy brighter dry conditions and can also be more tolerant of cold during the winter time.

What is common to all chilli plants is a need for warmth and light, and if our climate doesn't suit then we must do our best to mimic this in or around our homes.

For plants to grow and fruit successfully they ideally need to be kept in the range of 77-95°F or 25-35°C as much as possible from germination to picking. For most varieties this will be from early March through to August or September. In some places this is easy, but you might need to think about heated propagators and greenhouses. At lower temperatures plants will grow slower, be smaller and yields will be less.

Can I grow chillies where I live?

The chances are that wherever you live in the world you will be able to grow chillies somehow. If you live in the tropics or Mediterranean regions you could scatter a few seeds outside and, notwithstanding the usual climatic hardships and nasty pests, they would probably germinate and take care of themselves with a reasonable degree of success.

If you live in central parts of Europe, the UK or northern USA then, once again, you should be able to grow chillies easily, but you will need to pay extra attention to their warmth and wellbeing outside of midsummer.

In far northern and southern latitudes, you will need to recreate temperate or tropical conditions which will need a lot of forethought and planning to create a favourable artificial environment, but it is still possible to give your plants conditions in which they will thrive.

Is my house or garden suitable?

What you must always remember when it comes to growing chillies is that for most of us warmth and light are the most difficult challenges, and these challenges are most difficult to meet during spring time when you may need to create artificial warmth in order to give your seeds and plants the best start in life.

For some of us, warmth and light are two exclusive factors. The warmest place in our home might be above a radiator or in an airing cupboard, both of which might not benefit from the flooding light of a sunny window or conservatory. Conversely, those bright places around the home might be draughty or cold at night. Ultimately only you can decide whether you have a suitable spot, but the following tips will help you.

Temperatures

The germination of seeds happens best at temperatures above our usual room temperature of 70°F / 21°C. At room temperature, germination will happen, but it will be slower. You might also want to ask yourself how you can provide warmth around the clock; 'Our lounge window might be warm during the day but what about when we draw the curtains at night? And what about on dull days or times when we don't have our heating on?'

Light

Chilli plants don't necessarily need direct sunlight all day long, but they do need a good level of brightness to thrive.

Light is measured in units called 'lux'. Outdoors, the brightest sunny day could be up to 100,000 lux at midday and a bright area shaded from direct sun would be 20,000 lux at the same time. However, it is surprising to learn that a typical living room, when lit by a normal light bulb and a little extra from outside, might only be 150 lux, so clearly this wouldn't be enough to sustain our chilli plants, they would grow 'leggy', tall and flimsy, constantly reaching for light, the leaves will be pale and the plant won't be strong enough to bear fruit. Natural light falls by 50% for every metre you move away from a window. This helps us build up the picture that our plants need to be, at the very least, situated very close to a bright window, facing the sun, and preferably in a place where there is bright light coming from all angles. This either means outdoors, in a greenhouse, a conservatory or a large bay window. Don't let this put you off; a lot of pleasure can be gained from a single plant in a small window, but stick to something quick to make the most of a short season of brighter light, such as Apache or Cheyenne.

What about a greenhouse?

If you live in an area where temperatures aren't warm enough, or where temperatures can't be guaranteed, then a greenhouse or polytunnel is the finest alternative. As to the size of it, bigger is better. A larger air space will be less subject to big fluctuations in temperature and will maintain warmth for longer after the sun has gone. This is obviously not practical for lots of people, generally there are limitations such as space and cost, but any kind of protection is better than none at all so even the very cheap plastic greenhouses or covered shelves can be of help.

Glass Greenhouses

If you are lucky enough to have a glass greenhouse in your garden then make the most of this luxury. Even in areas where chillies grow well outside you can use the greenhouse to extend your growing season and to protect young and tender plants.

Where greenhouses are concerned that terrible phrase 'buy the best you can afford', comes to mind. The more space you can afford the better. Built-in staging (shelves) leave more growing and storage space beneath than ad-hoc benches. Toughened glass seems like a luxury at the time of purchase but, if you don't have it, one errant broom handle or a poorly aimed football and you will be wishing you spent the extra money. Ventilation is important to regulate the temperature in the height of summer and to stop mould growing in the autumn. Automated temperature controlled vents save you having to predict weather conditions if you are going out on a hot day. Whatever greenhouse you choose, one thing is guaranteed; it will always enhance your chilli growing experience.

Another luxury that will add huge benefits to your chilli growing hobby is a shelf-top heated greenhouse bed, usually constructed using a heating cable laid up and down a large tray of sand. Constant warmth rising up through your plant pots will ensure the best possible growth rate and even-out the cool spells between warm weather.

Polytunnels

Polytunnels (known as hoop houses in North America) are a relatively new addition to the domestic garden. The main advantage over a greenhouse is price, for a large growing space they are likely to be a fraction of the cost but also they have the added advantage of being less permanent so you can move them every few years to a patch of fresh soil. The disadvantage of a polytunnel when compared to a greenhouse is lack of ventilation. This can be combatted in various ways, larger tunnels have the option of roll up sides, or roof vents above the end doors. Unlike a greenhouse, a tunnel doesn't have to be erected on level ground, it can be positioned on a slope which means that on a hot day warm air rises from one end drawing cooler air in at the bottom, creating airflow at the same time.

In a polytunnel, you can easily grow your plants in the soil rather than pots, which has many advantages. A polytunnel, when managed properly, can be an amazing growing space providing a huge amount of food from a very small area, and the prolonged seasons you can gain from one will give you salad crops and root vegetables at times of year when you just wouldn't be able to grow them outside.

Plastic Greenhouses and Covered Shelves

These are often seen as a 'poor man's greenhouse', but the reality is that most of us can't afford the space or the cost of a glasshouse, so in that sense, these fill a gap in the market. They are also a natural choice for the beginner too. They won't stay as warm at night and because they don't have a great volume of air space they are subject to quick and extreme temperature changes. They also tend to lack ventilation and airflow so there is no harm in cutting some extra ventilation flaps in them; if you do so, put some strong wide tape where you are about to cut, then cut through the tape to stop the plastic tearing later on.

Self-Watering Systems

An automatic watering system is an easy halfway house between traditional growing methods and more complex hydroponic systems. There is really nothing negative to say about them, except for the added expense, if you have a large collection of plants.

The instant advantage of these systems is that they enable you to leave your plants unattended for up to a couple of weeks without worrying about watering them, great for midsummer holidays, often the downfall of the domestic grower.

Plants are set as normal in the pots provided and they are fed, by capillary action, from a reservoir of nutrient-enriched water which soaks up into the pots.

Hydroponics and Artificial Light

Hydroponic growing and artificial light are two ways in which people enhance their chilli growing or facilitate their growth where it wouldn't otherwise be possible. The skilled hydroponic grower will be able to guarantee a bountiful and continued crop without being tied to the seasons as a conventional grower would be.

An auto watering system – very effective for chilli plants, especially for growers that travel

NFT System, with chilli plants – this controls not only the watering and feeding but also root temperature

There is no need to jump into this with both feet, you can pick and choose which aspects suit your situation and adapt accordingly and, generally speaking, all this technology is very well suited to chilli growing.

The most popular and easiest way to enhance your growing experience is to use one of the many available self-watering systems or NFT (Nutrient Film Technique) systems. There are reasonably priced systems that run on a gravity or capillary supply of water and nutrients, and also more expensive ones which need an electricity supply but have the added benefit of regulating the root temperature and, hopefully, a quicker or better harvest as a result. The other obvious advantage is that, like the self-watering pots, the system can be left unattended for holiday periods.

These systems normally rely on a complete nutrient mix which you buy as a powder and mix with water.

Artificial Light

The second way of using technology to help with chilli growing is to use artificial light. A quick glance over the website of a hydroponic supplier will tell you that the amount of artificial light needed to sustain a single plant means the practicalities, and also the costs, are something to be reckoned with.

The lighting systems need to be suspended quite close to the plant, and it is only very recently with the advancement of LED technology that the heat generated by the bulbs, and the electricity consumed, has become less of a burden. LED lighting is now very much an option, but panels containing the hundreds of LEDs needed to provide enough light for larger plants are still expensive.

One area where LED lighting is of most help to the chilli grower is early in the growing season, when seedlings are contained in a small area and can easily be lit from a smaller LED panel. This is a good option for somebody who has little or no bright, warm window space in early spring time. If you choose to explore this option read very carefully into the capabilities of what you are buying to make sure it will be up to the job; it will always be an expensive indulgence.

CHOOSING WHAT TO GROW

Medusa – compact and suitable for restricted spaces but heatless

CHAPTER FOUR

Choosing What to Grow

A quick search on the internet will reveal hundreds, or even thousands, of varieties of chilli, and many of these can be bought as seeds to grow at home, but of all these varieties which ones will suit you best?

Firstly, you need to decide if there are any limiting factors in what you can offer in the way of growing conditions. Are you limited on space? Can you provide continued warmth for varieties that need a long growing season?

Secondly, what type of chillies do you want to grow? Do you want hot ones? Mild ones for the BBQ, or big ones for salads? Maybe you need specific types for specific recipes?

Hopefully you will already have been prompted into thinking about how and where you will grow your plants by earlier chapters in this book, and before you even picked up this book you will have had some thoughts as to what types of chilli you want to grow.

There are many dwarf varieties such as Medusa, Prairie Fire or Thai Sun which are bred for their compact size and are very suitable for window sill growing. When choosing varieties, it is worth remembering that as a general rule, the smaller the plant the smaller the chilli, and the hotter it is, although there are some, such as Medusa, which are deliberately bred to have no heat at all so they can be used as ornamentals in gardens where children play. So there aren't really any nice big mild chillies that grow on tiny bushes.

If it is your first time growing chillies then I would say avoid the record-breaking hot varieties. They have a very long growing season and will prove challenging in all but perfect conditions.

Whether you buy seeds from garden centres, by mail order or from the internet, the seller will normally give some indication as to how long a variety will take to ripen. This is often expressed in 'days from planting out' or 'days from potting on', which means the time period from small seedling of say 4-5 weeks old to first ripe fruit. This can mean anything from 60 to 130 days. So if you plant seeds at the beginning of March you could expect fruit from a very quick growing Apache plant by the middle of June. An Orange Habañero planted at the same time would not yield fruit until mid-August, so consider carefully about how long you think you will be able to nurture your plants and give them the warmth they need.

Variety Names

The names of chilli varieties can often be very confusing, sometimes misleading, and there are factors involved which deliberately try to confuse customers. The larger seed merchants often rename varieties to something more commercial, descriptive or flattering in order to tempt buyers into making a purchase. Subsequently, if the grower is happy with their results it ensures that, when they look for the same seeds next year, they will buy from the same company because the name they are familiar with isn't sold by anyone else. This confusion doesn't really exist when you buy from a specialist retailer of chilli seeds, but what you see in your garden centre often serves to confuse rather than help the hobby grower.

Also, beware that if a name implies the chilli is a hot one; don't necessarily take this as an indication of the true heat level. Words like 'Furnace' or 'Inferno' are sometimes misleading, so check the longer description on the back of the packet. If in doubt the picture is often a better guide. Remember the rule of thumb, 'the smaller the hotter'.

What makes things even more confusing is that the chillies you see for sale in supermarkets often carry a different name again, one that reflects its culinary use, its origin or its appearance. Seeds for these may only be available under a different name.

Chipotle is not a variety of Chilli

It is worth noting here that chipotle (pronounced 'chi-pote-lay') is a smoked chilli and therefore not something you can buy seed for. The word is from Nahuatl, a native Mexican language, and literally means 'smoked chilli'. Traditionally they can be made from any chilli, but usually they are made from Jalapeños, so, if it is chipotles you are after, then you need to grow Jalapeños and smoke them yourself (see the later section on smoking chillies).

Planning your Year

When choosing what to grow it is wise to take a moment to plan ahead and decide what you can realistically achieve with the facilities and temperatures available to you.

As an example, here is a rough guide to the lifecycle of an average Jalapeño plant based on a typical English summer.

1st March	Plant Seed.
10th March	Seedling emerges.
20th March	Pot seedling with its first 2 leaves into 10 cm pot.
25th April	Pot seedling with 6 or 8 leaves into a 25-30 cm pot and move it to its final home.
7th June	First flowers appear on the main stem, plant is now 30 cm high with side shoots starting to emerge from the main stem.
15th July	The first fruits are well formed; side shoots are bearing flowers themselves.
20th July	Pick the first few green chillies.
30th July	Plant is fruiting continuously.
15th August	If fruits are left on the plant they will now be turning red.
5th September	Plant will still be fruiting, think about moving it somewhere warmer to maintain fruit production.
1st October	Plant will start to die if not kept warm and sheltered.

This lifecycle is what you should be aiming for. In absolute perfect growing conditions things can happen more quickly, but the above timescale is more realistic. If your plant lags behind this schedule then you should think about what is going wrong, normally temperature is the culprit here. Less than satisfactory light levels, inadequate feeding and watering or mild pest damage will result in stunted or rambling and less healthy plants that bear a smaller crop, but they will still roughly conform to this timescale if the temperatures are right. If temperatures are too cool then plants will slow down or not grow at all and that is what drags things out for most people.

If you have grown chillies before and found they grow very slowly in the first few weeks of their life then there is always a temptation to plant them earlier than you did the previous year. Resist this temptation, they should grow vigorously in their first few weeks of life and, if they don't, then think about adjusting their living conditions rather than giving them longer to grow.

Plan what you grow to make sure you don't overstretch yourself and remember....

Key Point! *Don't plant seed too early if you don't have somewhere bright and warm to nurture your seedlings.*

Undersized Fruit in Cold Weather

Varieties of *Capsicum chinense* are particularly susceptible to cool temperatures and during a cold wet spell at the wrong time of summer their fruits may not develop properly. This results in some fruits ripening later without ever reaching their full size, (as a matter of course this is always noticeable among fruit that develop during late autumn). Where a chilli plant usually bears its biggest fruit first this could be reversed and those that develop in say a cold August might be smaller than those that form later. If this happens it is advisable to remove these early undersized fruits to promote growth of the rest of the crop.

Suggested Varieties

Here is a list of popular varieties; the 'time from seed to fruit' is the average time taken before the fruit can be picked. This usually assumes a germination time of 10 days or so and 6 weeks as a small seedling. For some varieties you need to wait until the fruit has matured to its final colour to make best use of it, whereas others, such as Pimiento de Padrón, Jalapeño or Hungarian Wax, can be picked earlier, and this is reflected in the fruiting time.

Key Point! *Don't buy varieties that take a long time to fruit if you don't have somewhere warm, bright and sheltered to keep them after the warmer summer months.*

Variety	Species	Time from Seed to Fruit	Plant Size	Fruit Colour	Fruit Size	Heat Level	Difficulty	Notes
Hungarian Wax	***Capsicum annuum***	16 weeks to yellow, 20 to red	Large & bushy	Green to yellow to red	12 cm	3-5,000 SHU	Easy	Used for stuffing, BBQs, salads and general cooking
Inferno	***Capsicum annuum***	16 weeks to yellow, 20 weeks to red	Larger & milder than Hungarian Wax	Green to Yellow to red	15 cm	2-3,000 SHU	Easy	Don't be misled by the name. Mild and used for salads and BBQs
Apache	***Capsicum annuum***	16 weeks to red	Small to medium & bushy	Green to red	2 cm	60,000 SHU	Easy	A general cooking chilli, easily dried
Jalapeño	***Capsicum annuum***	18 weeks to green, 22 weeks to red	Large	Green to red	5-7 cm	6-8,000 SHU	Easy	Used for pickling and general cooking. Traditionally smoked to make Chipotle
Serrano	***Capsicum annuum***	18 weeks to green, 22 weeks to red	Large	Green to red	3 cm	6-12,000 SHU	Easy	Used in general cooking and in Mexico for salsa
Prairie Fire	***Capsicum annuum***	19 weeks to red	Small & compact	Yellow to purple to red	1 cm	80-100,000 SHU	Easy	A good window sill chilli for easy heat in cooking
Pimiento de Padrón	***Capsicum annuum***	16 weeks to immature green	Very tall & bushy	Green (red if left)	3-8 cm	Mild	Easy	Picked immature for frying
Cheyenne	***Capsicum annuum***	18 weeks to orange	Short & Compact	Green to orange	4-6 cm	30-50,000 SHU	Easy	A heavy cropping general cooking chilli. A good single window sill plant
Poblano, or Ancho Poblano	***Capsicum annuum***	20 weeks to green, 23 weeks to red	Large	Green to red	12-16 cm	2-3,000 SHU	Moderate	Large, mildly spicy and good for stuffing
Twilight	***Capsicum annuum***	20 weeks to red	Medium & bushy	Yellow to purple to orange to red	1-2 cm	80,000 SHU	Moderate	A colourful display

Variety	Species	Time from Seed to Fruit	Plant Size	Fruit Colour	Fruit Size	Heat Level	Difficulty	Notes
Cayenne (many varieties)	***Capsicum annuum***	20 weeks to red	Tall	Green to red	8-12 cm	8-20,000 SHU	Moderate	Used for drying and general cooking
Joe's Long (Cayenne)	***Capsicum annuum***	20 weeks to red	Very tall	Green to red	30 cm	15,000 SHU	Moderate	Good for drying, but mainly grown as a spectacle
Thai Hot Demon	***Capsicum frutescens***	19 weeks to red	Compact & bushy	Green to red	1 cm	100,000 SHU	Easy	Prolific, easy to dry
White Habañero	***Capsicum chinense***	20 weeks to yellow / white	Compact	Green to yellow to creamy yellow	1 cm	500,000 SHU (unverified)	Moderate	Prolific, very hot and one of the quickest of the Habañero / Scotch Bonnets
Paper Lantern	***Capsicum chinense***	22 weeks to red	Large	Green to Orange	4 cm	250,000 SHU	Hard	Very prolific
Orange or Red Habañero / Scotch Bonnet	***Capsicum chinense***	23 weeks to orange/red	Medium & spreads wide	Green to orange or red	4-5 cm	200-350,000 SHU	Hard	Caribbean or general cooking and sauce making
Jamaican Hot Chocolate Habañero	***Capsicum chinense***	25 weeks to brown	Large & spreads wide	Green to brown	3-5 cm	600,000 SHU	Difficult	Caribbean and general cooking
Bhut Jolokia / Ghost Chilli	***Capsicum chinense***	25 weeks to orange	Large & spreads wide	Green to dark orange	4-7 cm	1,100,000 SHU	Difficult	Curry and very hot foods
Trinidad Scorpion	***Capsicum chinense***	25 weeks to orange	Large & spreads wide	Green to dark orange	4-7 cm	Up to 1,400,000 SHU	Difficult	Very hot Caribbean foods

See the Appendix for a few recommended seed sellers.

Jalapeño *– quick and easy to grow*

Apache *– compact, hot and very quick growing*

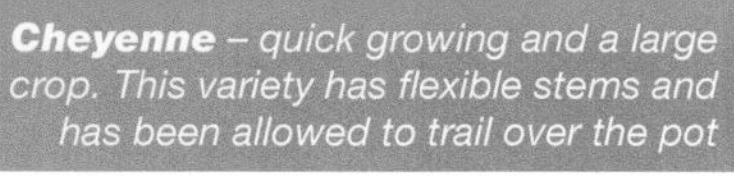

Cheyenne *– quick growing and a large crop. This variety has flexible stems and has been allowed to trail over the pot*

Inferno *– mild but prolific and versatile*

Bolivian Rainbow *– beautiful with multi coloured fruits and dark foliage*

Thai Hot Demon *– very hot and prolific*

Paper Lantern – an unusual but very prolific Habañero type, very heavy fruiting and reliable

Ancho Poblano – they may look like a sweet pepper but tastier and with some heat

Congo Trinidad Scotch Bonnet / Habañero – very hot but slow to mature and needs constant warmth

White Habañero – (the name is misleading; they are yellow and fade to cream) – this is a quicker growing Habañero, much smaller but hotter than typical orange or red

SOWING SEEDS

CHAPTER FIVE
Sowing Seeds

What Essentials do I Need?

Before you start, there are some basic essentials you will need to gather together for seed planting.

- Seeds!
- Small plastic pots of some kind, anything will do as long as they have drainage holes
- Soil suitable for seed sowing
- Labels, for identification
- Oh, and water

As well as these basics there are some not so essential things that will be of great help.

- Purpose-made small pots or trays
- Vermiculite
- A propagator, possibly electrically heated
- A max/min thermometer records highest and lowest temperatures since last reset

Soil

You should start your seeds in fine seed-sowing compost. I would use peat-free loam-based compost. There are many good quality composts available which don't contain peat, see the section on peat-free compost in the introduction. This should be fine, sandy and free of clumps and solid matter such as wood chips; these can cause problems if they block the seedling on its reach for the surface or if the roots try and grow into something other than soft soil. Some seed composts are surprisingly low quality so you may have to fish some bits out.

Once you have sown your seeds it is good practice to cover the soil with vermiculite; this is lightweight flakes of sterile water-retaining rock which traps moisture, allows airflow and inhibits the growth of mould.

Pots

What pots you use is very much a matter of space. Remember, the less you disturb your plants during their lifecycle, the quicker and healthier they will grow. If you have lots of suitable warm, bright space then you can afford to sow seeds individually into small (7.5 cm) or even intermediate (15 cm) sized pots. This will save time transferring them to bigger pots and will cause them less disturbance.

If you are limited for space then you can plant lots of seeds into a single pot then separate them when they are a week or so old.

Multiple Medusa seedlings germinated together through vermiculite

Small propagator with seedlings

Propagators

Unless the ambient temperature of your house is tropical or you have a convenient warm place, such as a shelf above a radiator, you would do well to purchase a heated propagator. These need not be expensive and don't have to be thermostatically controlled as long as you are careful. Place some capillary matting in the bottom (this is often supplied with the propagator) or alternatively cut a layer from a few sheets of newspaper. This will hold some moisture near the bottom of the pots and also helps dissipate heat from the heating element which may not be evenly spread across the bottom of the propagator, thus avoiding some of the seeds receiving more heat at the expense of others.

Be careful not to let your propagator overheat in direct sunlight especially if it is an electrically heated one, switch it off during the day if necessary and prop the lid open to allow extra airflow as soon as the seedlings start to emerge, the vents in the top aren't usually enough. Light is not crucial until the seedlings emerge but then it is vital they get plenty of light straight away.

When to Sow

You should really work backwards from a date when you think your conditions will be warm enough to move your plants into their final growing space, whether it is a greenhouse, garden or sunny window. Bear in mind that seeds will take a week or two to germinate and seedlings will be tender for the first 4 weeks or so of their life. In the UK, ideally you would want a sowing date of the beginning of March to give your plants the best possible chance, and earlier for some very slow growing varieties.

In ideal conditions they will grow quite quickly, and once the seedling has emerged they could be 15 cm tall with 8 or 10 leaves within 4 weeks, though 6 weeks is normal. If yours don't grow quickly then it is likely that lack of warmth is the problem.

Key Point! – *If you grew chillies last year but they were very slow don't fall into the trap of planting them earlier to give them a longer season. If they were slow there will be a reason for it, usually temperature.*

How Many to Sow

Usually you will have a packet of seeds with more than you need. All seeds from reputable seed merchants should have at least a 90-95% germination rate; they test part of the batch and shouldn't sell them if the germination rate is low. Therefore you should be able to rely on most of your seed germinating provided you treat them properly.

It is wise to plant more than you eventually expect to reach maturity as even the most vigilant grower might lose a few along the way. You can always give away any surplus plants to friends or swap them for something interesting. If you have plenty of seeds though, it is good practice to keep some back in case of disaster. If you don't use them this year, then provided you keep them cool and dry, they will keep until next year.

How to Sow

Whether you choose to plant one seed per pot or many, and whether you use pots, sets or trays, the rules are the same.

1	Remove any lumps from the seed compost and fill the container to within 1 cm of the rim.
2	Moisten the soil with water, either from a small watering can or a plant spray bottle. This way you won't need to water the seed as much after sowing and there is less chance of it floating to the surface.
3	Lay the seed or seeds on top, then cover with a thin layer of soil, just 4-5 mm is enough.
4	Vermiculite; this is always a good thing to use if you have some, but not completely necessary, cover the soil with 4-5 mm of it. This will help retain moisture and stop algae growing if the soil is damp.

This is all you need to do, place the pots in your propagator or warm spot and wait.

Warmth

Unless you live in a warm climate, room temperature isn't usually enough for a high germination rate and quick germination. You should aim for something higher. The range 75°F-85°F (23-30°C) is best. You will find the lower end of this range has a higher rate of germination and the higher end has quicker germination. The reality is, that temperatures are difficult to regulate except in laboratory conditions so aim for this range and your seeds should be happy. How you achieve these temperatures is down to personal preference, a propagator, heated or unheated, a boiler or airing cupboard (check them regularly) or a warm window are a few suggestions. If you do start them in a boiler or airing cupboard check them a few times a day and bring them into good light as soon as the first seedling starts to emerge to stop them getting straggly as they reach for light.

Watering

Do not waterlog your seeds; this will lead to mould and 'damping-off' (see later section on caring for seedlings). The chances are they will only need water once a day at the most and maybe much less, and only in small quantities as there is no big plant to dissipate the water through transpiration at this stage. Touch the soil or vermiculite with the back of your fingers, if it feels moist at the top then the rest will be fine. Vermiculite can dry on the surface and yet the soil can be moist. Lift the pot or tray; if it feels light and dry they probably need some water. Hold the pot up, if there is moist soil or condensation through the holes at the bottom then the seeds should be ok inside.

Germination

For most varieties planted in ideal conditions it will take from 7 to 14 days before you see a seedling emerge, sometimes quicker, and if yours are taking longer something is probably wrong.

Varieties with Erratic Germination

There are exceptions to this rule. Exceptionally hot varieties such as the Naga, Bhut, and Bih Jolokia and other varieties over 1 million SHU are well known as erratic germinators. This may be linked to their heat level, and research is being conducted into whether high levels of capsaicin inhibit germination.

Also, for some reason, those varieties that mature to a brown colour such as Jamaican Hot Chocolate Habañero and Ancho Mulato, always seem to be more temperamental than their orange or red counterparts.

Other varieties that can take longer are the 'wild' Tepin and Chiltepins (these are very close to the naturally occurring chillies from which modern varieties were bred).

The reason for these anomalies is probably genetic and if you grow any of these, be prepared to wait longer and prepare yourself for a lower germination rate too.

Seedlings emerging through vermiculite covered seed compost

Larger seedlings (5 cm)

Airflow

Good airflow is vital to guard against damp and mould. Whilst the seeds and the soil around them need to be moist there is no need for the rest of their environment to be dripping with condensation. Quite the opposite; the air will gain enough humidity from the moist soil and a dryer atmosphere will go a long way to stop the seedlings worst enemy, 'damping-off' (see next chapter). So as soon as the seedlings have started to emerge prop up the lid of the propagator or remove it all together to maximise light and airflow.

Oops! Nothing has happened

You should usually see some results from your planting within 14 days. If not then the two most common causes will be temperature or moisture. Do not despair, it doesn't mean they won't still germinate, they may well do, especially if they have just been kept a bit too cool, so persevere, but try and make an adjustment to the temperature if you can.

Moisture

If the seeds and soil have been allowed to completely dry out at a crucial time of their lives then there is probably nothing you can do. Imagine that a seedling could have emerged from the seed but before it shows itself above the surface the soil becomes parched and the seedling shrivels and dies.

Keep your seed compost damp and check it at least daily. If you are using a heated propagator check the soil in all of the pots or trays as the heat may not be evenly distributed and some areas may dry quicker than others.

Try Again

If your seeds don't succeed the first time then hopefully you still have some spare to try again. If you think you could have made an error then be vigilant and keep a watch on the temperature and moisture level. You could try keeping them somewhere different, maybe somewhere with less extremes of temperature. Also, don't throw away the first batch, they may still surprise you.

Growing Kits

There are many pre-packaged growing kits for chillies and other popular herbs or vegetables available to buy. Some of them provide a range of paraphernalia which is of particular help to the first time grower, and can be a reliable way of starting off your chilli plants, similar to the way this book describes. However, there are also some gimmicky ones which don't really give much of value apart from a few seeds, so check the contents list before you buy to make sure you are getting something for your money. See the Resources section for a recommendation.

Bulgarian Carrot

CARING FOR SEEDLINGS

Seedlings in trays of 6, each plug is 6 cm square

CHAPTER SIX

Caring for Seedlings

Pots and Soil

The best medium for bringing on small plants is soil-based compost rather than peat. A John Innes No.2 type peat-free substitute is best, but difficult to come by. A peat-free general purpose compost can also be used but be careful as quality varies; there are various online reviews that test the products of different manufacturers which may help in choosing a good one. It is good practice to lighten the soil by mixing in some perlite, an inert lightweight rock that traps moisture and helps to keep the soil aerated. Some compost you buy will already have perlite in, it is the white stuff you often see in the soil of potted plants and you can buy bags of it from garden centres.

If you intend to keep your plants in pots for the rest of their lives then there is no reason why you can't transfer small seedlings straight into their final larger pots as long as you have the space to keep them somewhere warm and bright. If the weather isn't warm enough for you to spread them out in your greenhouse or garden and you are stuck for space, then you should put them into trays of 6 or small (6 cm) pots for a few weeks. This is the normal route for most people, but involves an extra step in your plants' lifecycle as they will need to be transplanted again into bigger pots when they have about 6 or 8 proper leaves which will normally be after another 4 or 5 weeks.

Transplanting

Remember that you should try and keep disturbance of your plants to a minimum. If they have been planted with more than one seed per pot then you should separate them quickly into their own pots as soon as you can to avoid their roots becoming tangled with each other.

Always handle a small seedling by the leaves not the stem as they will have two leaves and only one stem and if you damage the stem the plant will probably die. Firstly, make a hole in the soil of the new pot using your finger or a small stick. Make it deep enough and wide enough to accommodate the roots of the seedling. Support the seedling by a single leaf but do not tug it. Carefully lift out the root with the surrounding soil using a spoon or similar implement and replant it into the bigger pot, then gently fill the hole around it. Carefully water it to wash the new soil in around the roots.

Light

As soon as your seedlings emerge they will start reaching for light. Within a couple of days you will begin to notice if they don't have the light they need to grow properly. They will grow long in the stem and bend towards the brightest light.

If you see your seedlings reaching in this way and becoming 'leggy' you should give them more light immediately, remove their propagator cover or put them in a brighter spot, even if it is only during the day. You can move them somewhere warmer at night.

A healthy seedling will not need to grow tall to reach for light

In darker conditions a seedling will grow indefinitely towards light until it finds the brightness it needs

Feeding

In the first 2 or 3 weeks after germination, your seedlings won't need any extra feeding. They will survive on the nutrients in the soil. After this they will need to be fed regularly with a liquid feed. When they are in small pots they will soon use all the nutrients available to them, especially if they are in particularly hot conditions and are being watered twice a day. Frequent watering will wash away the goodness from the soil quite quickly. Use a chilli or tomato plant feed according to the instructions on the bottle (see the later section on larger plants for a detailed explanation of plant feed).

Watering

This is a critical time for your plants. To start with, when they are small they won't be gobbling up the water from the soil so don't over-do it, moist is enough, not soggy. As they grow they will need more and more because they will soak it up more quickly.

Don't leave them standing in water, as their roots need some air and this will drown them.

When it gets to the stage where they need watering twice a day this is probably an indicator that they need to be repotted into something bigger.

Spraying or Watering in Sunlight

One cause of damage to plants which many people fall foul of is sun damage caused by water droplets on the leaves; it happens when you spray or water young, tender seedlings in direct sunlight. Each droplet can act as a tiny magnifying glass concentrating sunlight onto an area of leaf, leaving a small burnt dot the size of a pin head.

When this happens, often a lot of neighbouring plants or seedlings can be affected in the same way and the results can look like a disturbing disease or viral infection. This can be devastating, but as it only happens as a single event, if the plant isn't too damaged, then new growth will obviously not be affected. The way to avoid this is not to spray your plants during the day if it is sunny or there is a chance of sun before the moisture dries. They do benefit from a mist spray from time to time as explained in other parts of this book but for very young plants try to stick to mornings or evenings.

Oops! They all seem to be dying

This is the time when your chillies are at their most vulnerable and there are a few things that can happen that you need to beware of.

Damping-Off

Damping-off *– mould has caused some the seedlings to rot near the base and fall over*

Damping-off is the term used to describe an attack of soil-borne mould and bacteria around the base of the stems of newly germinated seedlings. It can also attack seedlings before they emerge from the surface of the soil. If your seedlings suddenly keel over as though they have been chopped at the base then this will be the cause. If you look closely you will see a small, brown, rotten mark at the base of the seedling.

The problem is most likely to occur in damp, low light conditions with poor airflow, just as mould would grow anywhere else.

To guard against damping-off do not leave seedlings waterlogged and make sure there is plenty of airflow and bright light. Once mould has set in amongst a group of seedlings there is little you can do to stop it spreading.

Sun Damage and Hardening-Off

Sun damage on a tender leaf, previously sheltered from direct sunlight

If your seedlings emerge in poor light and spend their first few days or even weeks away from any direct sunlight at all, then when you do expose them to sunshine you must be careful to do so in controlled conditions and, to start with, only for short periods of time.

When they are exposed to sunshine the leaves will, over a period of days, build up a waxy layer of protection on their surface. If you expose them to harsh sunlight before this happens the leaves will dry, curl up and eventually go brown round the edges or dry out completely. For a plant with only 2 or 4 leaves this is likely to be fatal.

If your seedlings haven't emerged into direct sunshine and become accustomed to it naturally, then, as soon as you can, expose them in the mornings or afternoons, or just for short periods during the day for the first few days.

You will see the leaves toughen and, on larger plants, they will feel thicker and waxy to the touch.

LARGER PLANTS

CHAPTER SEVEN
Larger Plants

What Essentials do I Need?

For larger plants these are the bare essentials you will need for successful growing.

- Pots or containers. They can be recycled containers; you can use anything as long as it has adequate drainage holes
- Liquid plant feed
- Soil suitable for planting

As for seed sowing, there are a few extras that may help you along the way.

- Purpose-made plant pots of a suitable size for your plant varieties (see below)
- A max/min thermometer records highest and lowest temperatures since last reset

Pots and Soil

If your plants are dwarf varieties that will remain compact, you can afford to keep them in smaller 15 cm diameter, 1 or 1.5 litre pots. Most chilli plants, however, can grow quite big. Plants grown in open soil in a greenhouse or polytunnel will often grow bigger than the advice on the packet suggests and some can reach 1.5 m tall and 1 m wide. Although it is often recommended that plants are kept in (relatively small) 20 cm (4 or 5 litre) pots I have found that plants tend to grow to the size of the pot and using something larger will get better results, provided you have the space. This is because plants kept in smaller pots will need much more attention to maintain an even level of moisture, nutrients and a regulated

Two Bulgarian Carrot plants grown in different sized pots, but with a similar feeding regime

Rows in an outside vegetable patch covered with weed control sheets. The white flakes are environmentally friendly slug deterrent.

temperature. In theory, you should be able to grow a large plant in a small pot by feeding and watering it regularly but this doesn't always happen and the plant suffers. They will be manageable in smaller pots for a while but when they grow large and start to support a large crop of fruit, a smaller pot will mean cramped roots that suck the soil dry very quickly in warm weather and will sometimes need watering twice a day. This does not make for ideal growing conditions and if the plant is left to wilt too much or too often it will shed flowers and new growth will be suppressed.

There is also the simple fact of stability to consider, plants can easily grow so big that a small pot doesn't give enough stability to stop it falling over, especially when the plant is laden with fruit. It is demoralizing to find that your pride and joy that you have nurtured for months has fallen over and broken one of its branches just for want of a bit of extra weight around the bottom.

Plants in a greenhouse bed

Growing in the Ground

If you have the facility to do so, then growing your plants in the ground, either outside if you have the climate or under cover, will usually give the biggest yields. As long as the soil is warm enough, the plants won't be subject to the big ranges in temperature and moisture levels that pot plants have to endure. Also, the roots can spread naturally and reach for fresh soil, so a regular feeding regime is less crucial.

Before you plant in the soil, whether it is outside or in a greenhouse or polytunnel, it is a good idea to check the soil temperature. It really needs to be over 66°F (19°C) before plants will grow healthily and preferably warmer, especially for *Capsicum chinense* (Habañero/Scotch Bonnet). To test the soil push your fingers a few inches under the surface, as the surface temperature will vary a lot throughout the day. If it feels warm to the touch then you will be ok, but if not then it might be worth investing in a soil thermometer so you can be more accurate. If your soil isn't naturally warm enough there are things you can do to help. Rather than planting in flat ground, heap the soil into mounds or rows. This increases the surface area facing the sun and soaks up more heat, much like a solar panel. Then cover the rows in black plastic or black weed control material so that they absorb more warmth from the sun and retain it for longer. This also helps by retaining moisture and suppressing weeds. You should then cut a cross in the covering where the plants are to go, space them about 45 cm apart.

Light.... again

Once again we come back to the subject of light. A healthy chilli plant should not look too 'leggy', its leaves should not be pale and the leaves should not be tender to the touch, they should be waxy and strong. If this is not the case then maybe your plant is lacking the light it needs, look back to the chapter on growing conditions for more of an insight into light quality and where a plant should be situated. Good light will help your plant grow healthily, increase the growth rate, the fruit yield and ripen the fruit more quickly.

Contrary to popular belief, chilli plants don't need full, direct sunlight all the time, especially in far northern or southern latitudes where day length could be as much as 18 hours. Plants in hot climates with harsh sunshine will even benefit from a little shade in the middle of the day, but this only applies if they are outdoors or in a greenhouse, and it is as much about the parching effects of the sun on the pots and soil as it is on the plant itself. In windows, where light is only filtering in from one direction they are already potentially deprived of part of the light they need so give them as much as you can. In a greenhouse, protecting small plants, especially *Capsicum chinense*, from too much harsh continuous sunlight is advisable. To diffuse the light but retain brightness you can hang white fleece or green shading from the inside of the roof. Polytunnel plastic tends to distribute harsh light anyway.

Feeding

You should get into the habit of feeding your plants regularly using either a dedicated liquid chilli plant feed or a liquid tomato plant feed. When the plants are fruiting you can almost feed them every time you water them. Follow the dilution instructions on the bottle.

Key Point! *Not feeding plants is a common reason for low yields or unhealthy growth.*

Poorly kept, light-starved plant, few fruit and no new flower buds

Why is some plant feed better than others?

Chilli plants do not need a lot of nitrogen, if they are fed too much then they produce lots of green leaf but take a long time to fruit, they may also drop their flowers if fed with a high nitrogen feed.

If you look on the back of a bottle of plant feed you will usually see a breakdown of 'N P K', this is amount of Nitrogen, Phosphorous and Potassium contained within. It is often illustrated in the format N4-P2-K7 or simply as numbers, 4-2-7. The 3 numbers vary from one product to another, and represent the proportion of each of the 3 elements.

As a very general rule of thumb, Nitrogen helps with foliage growth, Phosphorous for root growth, and Potassium is for fruit and flower formation. This is a very basic rule though as all three elements have other benefits. Of particular interest to the chilli grower is Potassium which helps guard against wilting during drought, heat and cold.

There are other nutrients involved in plant feed, but these main three help us to understand what type of feed a particular plant would need, for example, 'house plant feed' will be high in Nitrogen, so the first number will be high, as generally we want our house plants to grow leafy and green.

Beware of using too much manure in your soil if you are growing chillies outside, especially the un-rotted stuff as it is too high in Nitrogen. If you are growing chillies in the same soil for a number of years you will need to replenish the soil, but do so with well-rotted manure and condition it with general composted material.

Fed and Unfed Plants

The difference is obvious in these ***Medusa plants*** *– note the colour of the leaves; pale foliage is an obvious sign of malnutrition*

Inferno plants at 8 weeks from germination – although one has been fed and the other not, the nutrient content of the soil has sustained them both

At 16 weeks the difference between the same Inferno plants is obvious – the unfed plant on the left is smaller, paler and although it bears fruit there are fewer and there are no new flowers so it will not continue cropping until it is fed

Pruning

There should be no need to prune your chilli plants during the growing season. Some people think they should apply tomato growing techniques to chillies, presumably because they are commonly grown as glasshouse crops and their treatment overlaps, and therefore they should remove side shoots and growing tips. This isn't the case. As long as your plant is healthy and well fed it should flower and bear fruit from all or most of the nodes (where the stems branch) on the plant. So the bigger and bushier your plant the more it will produce.

If your plant looks like it is growing unnaturally tall and 'leggy' with the main stem flopping over then it is probably reaching for light and there is little you can do to limit that by pinching out the growing tip. It will not stop the plant growing tall as the side shoots will continue to reach upwards.

Some varieties have a taller habit than others, Cayenne, for example. These will naturally grow taller rather than broader, but again, pinching out the top will be of little help as the side growth will soon start to grow upwards. If your growing space is limited in height then make sure you choose a variety that has a lower, bushy habit.

Capsicum annuum flower

Flowers

Pollination

Chilli plant flowers are self-pollinating, that is, they don't have separate male and female flowers like pumpkins, for example. Chilli flowers are what is called 'complete', they have both male and female parts and pollen can be transferred from stamen to stigma within the same flower. Provided temperature and humidity are satisfactory (see below), then pollination can happen by wind, agitation or insect activity. It should not be necessary to bother with poking around in flowers with paint brushes or feathers to facilitate pollination. If there is any doubt as to whether a plant will pollinate then a good shake is usually enough. Remember that a large commercial grower won't be pollinating by hand and if they don't need to then neither do you. Other than that, with the possible help of insects, plants will take care of themselves. Having said this, cross pollination by insects can happen between other flowers on the plant or from flowers on other plants and this is normal too.

Flower-Drop

The occasional loss of flowers is natural and nothing to worry about. Especially with varieties that produce large numbers of tiny fruits, losing a few flowers will not affect the overall crop. There are circumstances when a plant will lose lots of its flowers, but these problems should be easy to remedy.

Humidity

Flowers need a humid atmosphere in order to pollinate successfully. If the air is too dry, satisfactory pollination won't happen and the unfertilized flower will drop off. This commonly happens on *Capsicum chinense* plants and the answer is to give them a daily mist spray and then give the plant a shake. In a warm greenhouse or conservatory it may also be possible to 'damp down'; water the floor with a watering can, which will bring up the humidity level without getting the plants too wet.

Nitrogen Levels

If a plant is fed too much nitrogen it will carry on producing leafy growth at the expense of fruit. This is a rarity, but it could happen if you are feeding your plant heavily with feed developed for houseplants, which is nitrogen-rich in order to make them big and green. It could also happen if you are fertilizing with something rich in nitrogen, like chicken manure. The good news in these circumstances is that, if you switch to a suitable feed, eventually you will have a much bigger plant and a bigger crop. Unfortunately this may be too late in the season for the harvest to ripen fully.

Heat and Cold

The other reason for non-pollination and flower-drop is extremes of temperature. A short period of too hot or too cold is not a problem as long as there is time in the brief lifespan of the flower to pollinate and the temperatures are not extreme enough to kill the plant. Ideally the flowers should not spend lengthy periods of time below 61°F or 16°C, or above 93°F or 32°C, though this varies slightly from one variety to another.

Fruit Development

The chilli (the fruit) develops behind the flower; technically it is the swollen fertilized ovary of the flower and the rest of the flower drops away as the fruit swells. Undersized, misshapen and seedless fruits are the result of poor pollination, and are most commonly seen during winter or late in the growing season or if the weather becomes too cold for healthy and effective pollination. Larger, healthy fruits, which contain a good amount of full sized seed, are the result of good pollination.

With a continued feeding regime your plants should carry on fruiting prolifically for as long as conditions allow. In a tropical climate, without significant seasonal temperature changes, they should carry on as perennial plants and fruit continuously, sometimes for years. As long as you keep picking ripe fruit regularly, your plants should fruit until the end of summer and those on the plant will ripen into the autumn.

The speed at which a fruit grows and ripens is dependent on the usual factors such as water, nutrition and temperature. Regular feeding is obviously necessary, but temperature and light are big factors, not only in general development but particularly towards the end of the season when you are waiting for colour changes to happen. Days are shorter, weather is unreliable and temperatures are lower. This is why I recommend some varieties as unsuitable for beginners; it is disappointing to find that after a summer of positive results you fail at the last hurdle because you don't have the means to keep longer maturing plants warm for that vital extra month in order to enjoy your harvest.

Newly developing fruit showing remains of flower petals

Capsaicin Levels: Can I make my chillies hotter?

The heat in chillies, the chemical capsaicin, develops as the seeds inside the chilli mature. The capsaicin is contained in plant cells that form the placenta, the strip inside the chilli to which the seeds are attached. They are packed full of the chemical and are fit to burst, so that if the seeds are disturbed in some way, the capsaicin sprays all over the seeds to protect them from being eaten by mammals (birds, with a less harsh digestive system, cannot detect the heat so they are a valuable way of spreading seed around).

Capsaicin levels increase with growing temperature, so chillies grown in a warmer environment will be hotter than those grown in a cool climate. You will notice this if you pick chillies from a plant that have developed in autumn or winter, they will still have heat but probably not as much.

Some people follow the reasoning that if a plant is stressed, by being starved of water, or subjected to very high temperatures to the point where the plant starts to die, then the fruit will be hotter. This has been proven to be true, but in chasing a small increase in heat you will sacrifice a lot in terms of quantity as a plant grown this way will be unhealthy and bear much less fruit. If you want extra heat then go for a hotter variety in the first place and grow the plant properly to maximize the crop.

Colour and Heat

There is no relationship between the colour of a chilli and its heat. The only rule of thumb that you can use to gauge heat without tasting a chilli is the size; smaller varieties tend to be the hottest (though this is not always true, a Habañero is bigger than a Birdseye, but hotter). A chilli that has ripened to red is not necessarily hotter than when it was green, or a red chilli hotter than a yellow, or for that matter an orange or black one.

A blackened Cayenne *– the black will fade back to green just prior to changing red*

What is Normal and What Isn't?

My chillies are going black!

Some varieties, especially Jalapeños, Serranos and Cayennes are susceptible to black (in fact a very dark purple) discolouration of the fruit at certain stages of their growth and at the joints of plant stems. This is quite normal and nothing to worry about. It usually happens to the part of the fruit that is most exposed to the sun. The stems will stay black, but the fruit will eventually change colour again, back to green and then to red. The chemicals that cause this phenomenon are Anthrocyanins, they are what gives purple colour to plants and fruit, and also act as a sunscreen. Some *Capsicum annuum* chilli varieties produce this chemical naturally to protect the fruit in areas most exposed to sunlight. It is not desirable in fruits grown for supermarket sale so some plant breeders have produced varieties that don't do it, but others have taken advantage of the trait and bred chillies such as Purple Jalapeño and Royal Black, which take the discolouration to an extreme and produce a stunning plant with purple or nearly black leaves and fruit.

Purple Flash *– a beautiful variegated plant. The curled white leaves are perfectly natural*

Variegated Plants

Of the thousands of varieties of chilli plants available, some of the most interesting are the variegated ones. These are commonly bred to have dark purple or black foliage, or the usual green, but all of which have pale green or white streaked leaves. The pale contrasting part of the leaves can also wrinkle or curl giving the impression of disease, but for varieties such as Tricolour-Variegated, Purple Flash and Fish Pepper (which also has streaked fruit) this is quite normal. You may also see variegation in normal chilli plants from time to time, it is a genetic aberration which occurs naturally and it is this variation that has sometimes been exploited to develop new and attractive varieties.

Corking

On some varieties, especially Jalapeño and Serrano, when the fruit starts to mature you may see a web of scarring on the skin. This is quite normal and a sign that the chilli is ready to be picked, regardless of colour.

Ripe, green Jalapeño displaying characteristic corking

Harvest Time

When to Pick

With the exception of Pimientos de Padrón, which are deliberately picked immature to be fried and eaten whole, chillies are ready to be picked once the seeds have developed inside, regardless of colour. It is simply a matter of personal taste or purpose that dictates picking time.

All chillies will change colour during their development, and this colour change only happens once they are ripe, so if they have changed colour then they will definitely be ready to pick. Most start green and change to red, orange or yellow, but some start black or yellow, and some go through 2 or 3 colour changes.

Ripeness before a colour change is obviously more difficult to detect without chopping a chilli open to look at the seeds but there are a few tips which will help. Generally speaking, chillies appear slightly dull, soft and sometimes ridged while they are immature, some more so than others. Once the seeds start to develop inside, the fruit fills out and becomes firm and the dull appearance turns to a glossy one. Give one a squeeze and feel or hear it crunch inside, this is a good indication that it is ready. Each different variety has its own characteristics, so with the first one or two you pick off a bush it will be trial and error as to whether they are ripe enough, but you will soon learn to identify the ripe ones.

How to Pick

You should pick the chilli and its stalk off together. You will find a ripe chilli will snap naturally where the stalk joins the stem of the plant. Some tougher types such as those of the *Capsicum baccatum* species might need a good tug, but mostly just a flick of the fingers will do it.

If you are picking in bulk and are going to process your chillies in some way, such as sauce making, then you might find it saves time to pick them without stalks, break them where the stalk joins the chilli leaving the stalk on the plant. You will not get stung by the heat when picking unless you break open the chilli, the outside is safe to touch.

Don't Delay Picking

Throughout this book you will often see pictures of chilli plants bearing lots of ripe, colourful fruit. A heavily-laden chilli plant makes a fantastic spectacle, an interesting conversation piece and you will be the envy of your friends. However, you will reap greater rewards if you pick your chillies as soon as they ripen rather than leaving them on the bush. Much like dead-heading ornamental flowers, the plant is encouraged to set new fruit by removing what is already there and your overall crop will be much more bountiful.

> ***Key Point!*** *Picking chillies as soon as they ripen will encourage the plant to produce more and your overall crop will be bigger.*

This is a trick used by commercial growers of chillies and peppers. Picking and selling them green will get them more of a crop, and therefore more profit per plant than leaving them to go red, which takes a lot longer, even though consumers may find red peppers more desirable.

Whatever stage you choose to pick your chillies, don't leave them on the plant longer than you have to. If you don't need them straight away, freeze them or dry them, but make sure you maximize your crop.

PESTS, DISEASES & OTHER PROBLEMS

CHAPTER EIGHT

Pests, Diseases and Other Problems

Me!

The famous organic gardener Bob Flowerdew once said;

> *'Seeds want to come up, plants want to grow, flower and fruit, all we have to do is not do anything that stops them.'*

For the most part, plants are grown in an artificial environment over which we have control. This makes them our babies; largely dependent on us for all that they need to survive. So before you go down the route of trying to apportion blame to some invisible disease, or things like seed quality, ask yourself the simple question. Have I really given my plants the things they need to flourish; warmth, light, water and food? If the answer to any of these is no, and your plants are looking discoloured or generally unhealthy, think about this before apportioning blame to disease.

Having said this, there are a few other common problems which may be very easily diagnosed.

Biological Control of Pests

For most of the invertebrate pests (bugs, slugs and snails) you will come across, there are biological controls available from internet or mail-order companies and some larger garden centres which will help you in your battle. These are naturally occurring invertebrates or bacteria which prey upon your pests, either by eating them or infecting them in some way. For most of the pests described in this book there is a natural biological control listed as a means of controlling them. If you use these, you will often just be supplementing something that occurs naturally in the soil or outside environment, so they are a very eco-friendly means of pest control.

Companion Planting

Companion planting is all about making the most of the natural abilities of some plants to either attract or deter insect predators and sometimes diseases too. This is a complete subject deserving of a book all of its own, but there are a few plants worth mentioning that will definitely benefit the chilli grower. The first are Alliums, the onion and garlic family. These are a great deterrent to greenfly (aphids), the bane of the chilli grower's life. The second are plants like tansy, marigold, coriander and borage, which attract insects such as hoverflies and lacewings that predate upon other pests. Of all the companion plants maybe the most obvious to the chilli grower are coriander and garlic as they are both beneficial to chilli plants and will complement the use of chillies in the kitchen too. Growing these plants around your vegetable patch, patio or greenhouse has obvious benefits all-round.

Overwatering

Unfortunately, the symptoms of overwatering are very similar to the symptoms of under-watering, a wilting and sorry·looking plant.

It is quite natural for a plant to look slightly droopy during or towards the end of a long day in the sunshine and this isn't necessarily an indication of ill-health. If, however, the plant is permanently wilted then this is more of a problem. There are other diseases mentioned later that may be the cause of this, but it is most likely to be simply too much or too little water. The rule of thumb is that if the plant is wilted early in the day and the soil is dry then it definitely needs watering. Feed it too, to give it a boost. Waterlogged soil starves the roots of vital oxygen, so if the soil is wet, resist the urge to water it again and leave the plant until the soil begins to dry out. If the plant is still wilting then disease is likely.

> ***Key Point!*** *Continuing to water an already waterlogged plant because it is wilting is a common mistake that beginners make.*

Slugs and Snails

This is probably the most common problem that befalls chilli plants grown outside, and it isn't just the leaves they are after.

Slugs and snails love chilli plants. If a single, unprotected pot of germinated seedlings is left vulnerable in a greenhouse, then a small mollusc can eat the whole lot in one night.

Curved sections eaten out of leaves, or even missing leaves and stems are a tell-tale sign that a slug or snail has been at work. But they don't stop at this.

At this point, it is worth explaining something about capsaicin, the chemical that gives the 'heat' to chillies. It is only detectable by mammals, and even some of them don't

A slug eating a chilli plant leaf

A snail attacking tender new growth

Evidence of old slug or snail damage *– the chewed edges have turned brown*

Snail damage on an un-ripe Big Bomb *– snail damage around the top of a chilli is common*

worry too much about its deterrent qualities. Birds, reptiles, fish, and, most significantly, insects and other invertebrates don't detect it at all. It is a common misconception that because chillies cause us humans a degree of discomfort then other creatures will be put off by it; some people imagine slugs and snails frothing on contact with a chilli as they would with salt. This is absolutely not the case, and they happily chomp their way into a nice, juicy chilli and enjoy every second of it.

The first step you should take with slugs and snails is prevention. Try and minimise their possible hiding places. Whether your plants are kept outside or in a greenhouse, the same advice applies. Keep weeds to a minimum, remove all unnecessary pots, trays and debris from the surrounding area, if your plants are in pots then check underneath them regularly, this is the most common hiding place for slugs. Flat surfaces away from direct light are the favoured place for snails.

What to do when you find them is a matter of personal choice; remove them to a far off place and release them alive, toss them over the fence into a neighbour's garden (please don't consider this as a serious alternative!), or drop them into a bucket of salt, are all options. A simple and satisfactory stomp is my preferred method but some people aren't comfortable with this and if you do, be careful, as a mass cull can make the soles of your boots very slippery.

Slugs breed and hide in open soil, burying down in dry weather. If you grow your plants in an open vegetable plot or in soil beds in the greenhouse then you should try one of the many brands of nematode applications such as NemaSlug®, which is available by mail order or from garden centres. These are powders containing nematodes (microscopic parasites) that prey upon slugs, laying their own eggs in the slug's body so their offspring devour it from inside. They are normally applied in late spring, as they work best when the soil has started to warm. The product is diluted in a watering can and sprayed over your growing plot according to the instructions. You are really just boosting the population of an organism that lives naturally in the soil anyway, and one application will provide a living population of the nematodes that will last throughout the season.

If you still have a problem, then one or more of the other remedies might suit your situation. You can spread a ring of salt around your pots, or use copper bands available from garden centres which carry a minute electrical charge that deters molluscs. Some people swear by beer traps; strategically placed saucers of beer will attract slugs and snails which then fall into the liquid and drown in a drunken stupor, not a bad way to go.

If you choose to use slug pellets then please be careful. There are environmentally friendly ones available now which are not damaging to other wildlife, but you should follow the instructions carefully and, if you use poisonous pellets, make sure the pellets themselves as well as the dead bodies of poisoned slugs are not accessible to wildlife or pets that might accidentally be poisoned.

As a last resort, you will have to go to the front line of the battle ground and tackle them as they start to launch an attack. This means going out around an hour after dark with a torch to try and catch them before they start to munch. Look around pots, in the tops of new growing stems and under leaves.

Greenfly and Blackfly (Aphids)

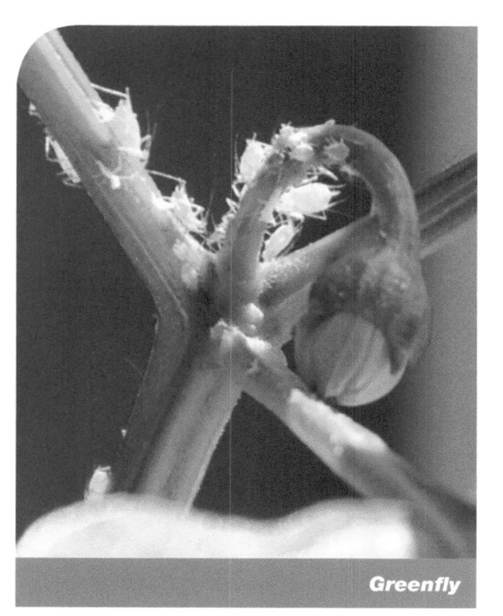

Greenfly

Greenfly and blackfly are general names for many different types of aphid. They live by sucking the sap out of plants and chilli plants are particularly vulnerable. They can drain a plant of its vitality and also spread disease.

Greenfly have a complicated and bizarre lifecycle. They don't need to mate to have babies, females can be born pregnant, and depending on prevailing conditions, they can be born with or without wings.

As a grower, you need to be able to identify them and also read the signs of their presence even before they become noticeable themselves.

Sometimes it is a mystery how greenfly and blackfly materialise. They can drift in on air currents from hundreds of miles away, or they can hibernate in leaf litter in an untidy greenhouse or garden.

The first sign of greenfly is a sticky leaf surface or tiny white shed skins often misidentified as whitefly.

Another sign of a past or current greenfly infestation is curly or malformed leaf shoots where the greenfly have attacked the tender parts of a plant and left scarring which only becomes evident during later growth.

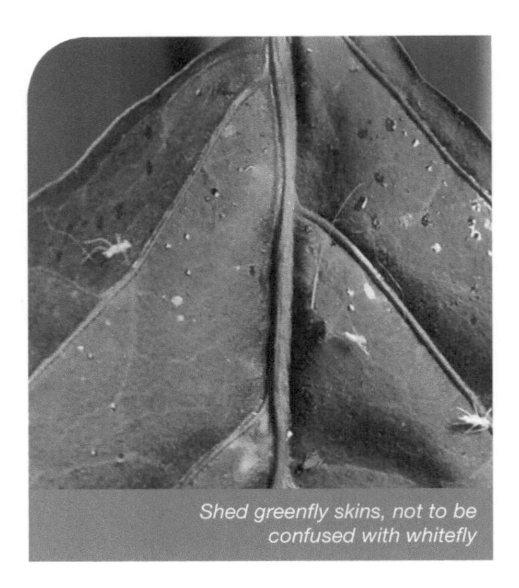

Shed greenfly skins, not to be confused with whitefly

There are a number of ways of dealing with greenfly and blackfly. It may sound unsavoury, but crushing aphids by hand is an effective way of reducing the population, especially if there are only a few, but inevitably you won't squish all of them, and those remaining will breed again but this should be your immediate line of attack.

Greenfly

The most romantic and the most effective way is to use ladybirds. Collect them from around your garden or immediate locale and place them on your plants. They live on aphids and can eat around 40 a day. Their voracious larvae (offspring), which are completely unlike the adults, are even more effective. The larvae look like tiny, blue-grey dinosaurs and march around quickly preying on juicy aphids as they go.

Ladybirds can be difficult to find in some summers, look among stinging nettles, a favourite host plant of greenfly, or in long grass and meadows.

The traditional method of killing aphids is spraying with mild, soapy water. They breathe through their skin and the soap washes water into their breathing pores and they drown. Be careful with this method though, as many modern soaps such as washing-up liquid contain antiseptics and other chemicals which will damage or kill plants.

There are a number of commercially available organic sprays which will also do the job, they contain natural insecticides made from plant extracts which will be safe to use on your plants as you don't want to contaminate what you will eventually be eating.

If you are growing a large collection of chillies under cover, you may wish to use a biological control called Aphidius (see resources section). These are tiny

Malformed leaves due to earlier greenfly infestation

Ladybird larva; the best controller of aphids – the white flies are actually the shed skins of greenfly

wasps that look more like little flies and they lay their eggs in greenfly, then their larvae eat the inside of the greenfly, and it dies. They won't eradicate a bad aphid infestation, but if they are present from the start they will keep on top of them and stop a population explosion.

Whitefly

Whiteflies are a type of bug sometimes found among greenhouse crops, particularly tomatoes. In a domestic setting, the diagnosis of whitefly is often a wrong one as people see the shed white skins of greenfly and assume them to be whitefly. They can attack chilli plants, and the way to rid your plants of an infestation is similar to the procedures you would use for greenfly, they can be killed with an organic pest control spray. The biological control for whitefly is lacewings; the delicate long, green insects with transparent wings seen flying in summer. You can collect them or buy them, and both the adults and larvae are voracious eaters of whitefly and greenfly (see resources section).

Caterpillars and Grubs

There are a number of caterpillars or insect larvae that may infest your chilli plants. The good thing about caterpillars is that, unlike greenfly and other smaller insects, they usually only have one lifecycle in a season and therefore aren't necessarily a recurring pest, so once you have got rid of them they are less likely to return. They can still, however, be devastating; caterpillars grow quickly and can overcome a plant in just a few days. The damage is not always limited to leaves; they will also eat around the join between the fruit and the stem and sometimes the flesh of the fruit itself.

Moth caterpillars and their droppings on a chilli plant

A caterpillar attacking the flesh of a chilli at night

At first glance, the evidence of their presence might be misdiagnosed as slug or snail damage, but there will be additional evidence in the form of round, black or dark green droppings, known as frass, on or below the leaves. The first line of attack should be to examine the plant and try and eliminate them by hand. They are usually quite well disguised, but often lie along the veins of leaves or along the edge of the damaged eaten areas. You can flick them off by hand and crush them or give the plant a shake and catch them after they have fallen to the ground. If you can't find them during the day time then return when it is dark and you will be more likely to catch them feeding. Some species roll themselves up in the edge of a leaf; these are easier to spot and deal with.

Again, there is a biological control available for caterpillars in the form of a powder containing bacteria that can be diluted and sprayed onto the plants, but this is more suited to commercial greenhouse growing where there is a resident population that breeds repeatedly throughout the year. I would recommend dealing with them by hand, or with a general organic insect pest spray.

Red Spider Mite

You will see evidence of red spider mite before you see the actual pests themselves. They thrive in dry greenhouses and conservatories and are very dependent on a hot dry environment, in such conditions they will undergo a population explosion in just a few days.

You are much more likely to experience red spider mite if you also grow cucumbers, pumpkins, melons or aubergines as these are more common targets than chilli plants.

The first symptoms are pale, yellowing leaves and, eventually, fine dusty webs and, if you look closely, millions of tiny crawling bugs, which, to the naked eye, aren't even very red. The leaf discolouration is very similar to nutrient deficiency, but if you look closely the discolouration will be accompanied by a slight dustiness on the leaves. There are sprays and biological controls for red spider mite but the first course of action is to spray the affected area with water, this inhibits population growth as they hate moisture and humidity. Once you have experienced red spider mite in your greenhouse or conservatory, the chances are it will return year after year unless you are careful. You will need to thoroughly clean and disinfect during the winter to try and stop them, as they hide in cracks and crevices. Do not confuse red spider mite with the larger, brighter red mites (2-3 mm) that you sometimes see singly in hot greenhouses and around the garden, these may well be Phytoseiulus, a predator of the red spider mite and a friend to the chilli grower.

Fungus Gnats

These are small black flies usually seen around house plants, particularly older ones where the soil is no longer sterile and there is leaf matter rotting into the soil. They are often confused with blackfly, the black aphids, but their habit is quite different. Blackfly are sticky and amass around the tender parts of a plant. Fungus Gnats are much more active and annoying as they are constantly flying around the plant. The adult flies are just that, an annoyance, but the grubs are more damaging as they will eat tender roots and eventually the plant will start to lose its vigour.

The way to rid your plant of these flies is to break the lifecycle by killing adults and larvae. If you hang sticky fly paper near the plant it will trap adults. At the same time let the surface of the soil dry out and lay a slice of raw potato on the surface. This will act as a food source and attract the grubs which will burrow into the potato and it can then be discarded. Then, if possible and without damaging the roots, scrape away a layer of soil from the top of the pot and replace it with an inch or two of fresh sterile potting compost. If this is rough coir compost then even better, this is too rough for the grubs to thrive in. There are also chemical insecticides you can add to water to combat these flies too, check the label to make sure it is suitable for edible vegetable crops.

Viral, Bacterial and Fungal Infections

Bacterial Spot

Bacterial spot

This is probably the most common infection you are likely to see on your chilli plants. It starts with moist spots on the underside of the leaves which quickly spread through the leaf to the top surface leaving a pale brown patch, often with a red-brown edge. Eventually, the leaf will turn yellow and drop off, and the disease can affect the chillies themselves too. It is easily spread in water droplets so it favours damp humid conditions such as an over-crowded greenhouse. It can be transmitted through infected seed but is most likely to occur in leaf litter and dead plants where it will continue to grow. The remedy in a domestic environment is to remove infected leaves, or even infected plants, and destroy them. Maintain good airflow and guard against damp conditions and wet foliage.

Blossom-End Rot

Blossom end rot

This is an easy problem to diagnose, but a more difficult one to solve. Long, fleshy chillies and sweet peppers are most susceptible, and the symptom is a necrotic lesion at or near the tip of the fruit. In a damp situation the diseased area will spread and the fruit will be useless. In a drier environment the lesion may dry up and leave a scab and the fruit may survive, albeit damaged. The direct cause of the problem is a lack of access to calcium. This can be because the soil itself is lacking in calcium, and if all of the chillies on the plant suffer throughout the growing season, then this could be the cause. More commonly the problem is caused by erratic watering and spells where the soil dries out at a crucial time during the fruit's development and the plant can't take up calcium, even though the soil itself isn't lacking. Likewise, the plant finds it difficult to take up nutrients if the soil is too wet. If you are growing plants in open soil then you are less likely to see blossom-end rot, but if you grow big, long, fleshy chillies in pots then drying out of the soil can be a common occurrence and this is likely to be the cause.

Verticillium Wilt

Verticillium wilt is a mainly soil-borne fungal infection that infects the plant via root infection. The symptoms, as the name suggests, are wilting leaves, but initially it is often only one side or one part of the plant that is infected as the infection spreads up through the vascular system (the flow of liquids through the plant) from the origin of the initial infection in part of the root system. You are unlikely to see Verticillium wilt among potted plants unless you use unsterilised soil taken from the ground outside, as it affects a wide range of plants, both cultivated and wild. Because the initial symptoms are wilting, the disease is often unnecessarily blamed when over or under-watering is the cause. In an outside vegetable patch or in a polytunnel, the way to avoid the disease is good plant husbandry; do not leave rotting plants around at the end of the year. If you have suffered an attack then rotate crops so that you aren't growing susceptible plants in the same soil the following year and do not leave the plants waterlogged.

Tobacco Mosaic Virus

This is a viral infection which affects a lot of greenhouse crops, but you are unlikely to see it if you only have a few plants at home. The symptoms are yellowing between the veins of the leaves in young growth, followed by a mosaic of patchy discolouration. If you see symptoms like these, the most likely culprit will be malnourishment due to infrequent feeding, or possibly the early signs of red spider mite.

Phytophthora Blight

This is another fungal infection which takes hold when plants are kept in cramped, humid conditions with little airflow, and where rain or overhead watering means the leaves do not get a chance to dry properly. The symptoms are wilting leaves and wet lesions on the stems. Remove infected plants immediately and destroy them. To guard against this disease do not waterlog the soil and rotate crops if the disease takes hold.

Sunscald

Sunscald is something that doesn't normally happen unless there is another factor involved besides sunshine. The plant can suffer from sun damage (dry parched leaves), but this is normally prompted by wilting due to lack of water, or where young plants have suddenly been exposed to strong and direct sunlight for the first time, a healthy plant isn't normally damaged by sunshine.

Sunscald on a young, tender chilli

The symptom of sunscalded fruit is a yellowing patch of softness, as though it has been exposed to a grill. The damaged area soon goes rotten and mouldy. This happens if a young fruit has been suddenly exposed from under leafy foliage or where heat has built up as a result of being pressed against the glass of a greenhouse or window. Pick off the affected fruit and throw it away.

Mice

Capsaicin and chilli powder is sometimes used as a deterrent against animal damage; farmers use it to protect crops from elephants in Africa, and people who feed wild birds use it to protect peanuts from squirrels; and, of course, for some humans chilli is none too pleasant.

Don't be fooled into thinking that this will protect the fruits of your hard labour from rodent pests though. Mice love seeds, and there are two stages of your plants' growth when they will be vulnerable.

The first is when seeds have just been planted. If you have a problem with mice in your greenhouse or garden they may dig up the seeds and eat them. Evidence of these excavations will be obvious.

Secondly, and altogether more audaciously, they will attack fully ripened chillies and gnaw into them to get at the seeds inside. They somehow sense that there are bigger seeds in bigger chillies and that is what they prefer, but if there are no large chillies or peppers available then they will go for whatever is next and if that means eating their way into the hottest chilli in the world then that is what they will do.

Be wary about mice, their population level is greatest at the end of summer and when nights start to get colder they seek the warmth of polytunnels and greenhouses. This is the time when chillies are likely to be ripe for the picking and they can cause serious damage in just one night. On a small scale, traps are best, if you use poison follow the instructions rigidly and wash any fruits picked from nearby.

Mice won't attack immature chillies as the seeds won't have formed so try and pick fruits as soon as they are ripe or the mice might get there first.

KEEPING PLANTS OVER WINTER

CHAPTER NINE

Keeping Plants Over Winter

Some Varieties are Better than Others

If you are considering trying to keep your plants over winter then it is worth bearing in mind that some varieties stand a better chance of survival than others.

Generally, bigger, fleshy chillies that grow on big plants with large, fleshy leaves won't do as well as a tougher, woody stemmed, small leaved plants.

This means that varieties like Poblano, Wax Chillies, Inferno or sweet peppers aren't good for keeping over winter. Not only are they less likely to survive, they are also fairly quick growing and so there is less benefit in keeping them. The real benefit is to keep slower growing plants so that you get a head start in spring time and an earlier crop next year.

Various varieties of Aji (*Capsicum baccatum*), Hot Chocolate Habañero, Tepin, Tabasco, and small Thai chillies are more likely to survive and will also reward you with an early crop next year.

Temperature

Ideally, chilli plants shouldn't spend anything longer than short periods below 61°F or 16°C. They can tolerate occasional periods of near freezing temperatures but you shouldn't take this for granted and if these periods last for more than a few hours, or occur on a nightly basis, then your plants won't survive.

In the UK, this means you will need to bring your plants indoors in September or October in order for them to survive. Even a greenhouse or garage will not be warm enough unless it has heating. This often leads to life or death dilemmas when there are just too many plants for the space available. Which one stays and which one goes?

Feed and Water

Keep the soil slightly moist, but bear in mind that in cooler temperatures the leaves will not transpire as much and therefore the plant won't suck up as much water as in the summer so less frequent watering is the order of the day, maybe as little as once a week.

Re-potting

A few months of regular watering from above can cause the soil to settle and become compacted, which closes out vital air gaps and stops oxygen reaching the plant roots. As the plant has taken up a lot of the nutrients from the soil it can become too acidic which will suppress growth in the coming year.

It is therefore worthwhile re-potting the plant before it starts to grow again at the end of the winter. Loosen the soil slightly around the roots to provide aeration, put it into a bigger pot with some extra fresh soil and give it a feed. It should start shooting out in early spring and show quick and healthy growth, bearing fruit earlier than in its first year.

Pruning

This is a difficult topic to advise on and very much needs some judgement on your part. Let's go back to our earlier discussion on the natural environment of chilli plants. Some people grow plants where they can enjoy tropical conditions all year round; living in the tropics helps, and in these conditions, your plants will continue growing for a long time, they know no seasons and flourish as long as they are fed and watered. If you don't live in the tropics but have a nice, bright, heated conservatory then your plants might do the same. In which case you need to do nothing more than enjoy a continuing supply of fresh chillies.

If your conditions are less than ideal, then your plants will reflect this. Cooler temperatures and less light will mean they may become dormant, lose their leaves or die completely. If your plant starts to die back you should prune it into shape, removing any dead stem tips or if the stems start to die completely then cut it right back to a few strong woody stems and it should shoot out when temperatures start to warm again.

Removing Fruit

Your plant will slow down or even stop growing over the winter time. Any fruit that it may bear are likely to be stunted, lacking in heat and with little flavour. Therefore it is best to pick them off so they don't sap energy from the plant unnecessarily.

WHAT TO DO WITH YOUR CHILLI CROP

CHAPTER TEN

What to do with Your Chilli Crop

Although this is a book about growing chillies and not a recipe book, it is common amongst chilli growers to get a little carried away with their hobby and end up with a lot more chillies than they know what to do with. This chapter gives a few tips on the common ways of preserving your chillies for future use in cooking.

Freezing

Freezing is generally the easiest way of preserving chillies, and one which lots of people overlook. The only downside to this is if you need them to remain crisp for use raw, such as in salads, as they will go soft when they thaw.

There is no need to blanch or treat them in any way, just freeze them whole. It is good practice to keep a bag in your freezer and whenever they ripen on your plants you can just throw them in. They won't stick together and you can take them out one by one when you need them.

Chop them from frozen, by the time you put them in your cooking they will be thawed.

Drying

Chillies drying in a sunny window

Drying is a traditional method of preserving, and some varieties lend themselves to it more than others. In fact, some are grown almost exclusively for this purpose. It tends to be longer, thin fleshed ones such as Cayenne that dry most easily, some are quite dry and leathery on the bush before you pick them.

Others such as Habañeros have a waxy coating and won't dry at all unless you crush or slice them first to allow the moisture out. If you do so, they must be dried quickly before they go mouldy.

If you have somewhere you can dry chillies it is worth trying. Although the heat level will stay the same flavours can change when they dry and become richer and less fruity. Flavours can be reminiscent of other dried products, with hints of raisins, sultanas, tea, chocolate or tobacco.

In arid climates chillies are simply laid out to dry in the sun or strung up in 'ristras' to dry in the wind. This may not be practical; certainly in the UK, conditions suitable for drying this way are almost unheard of, especially as we will probably be picking red chillies towards the end of the summer or into the autumn when nights are cold and damp.

So for many of us, this leaves us with having to dry our chillies indoors. For very small or thin chillies this can be as simple as leaving them on a tray in a sunny window. They can also be lined up along the top of a double radiator or above a heater. Anywhere warm will do, in front of an open fire, next to an Aga® cooker, a boiler or in an airing cupboard.

There are commercially available, domestic food driers which can be used for other foods too, like sliced apples, apricots and beans.

Chillies strung in a 'ristra' for drying

Smoking

Chipotles *– in this case smoked Jalapeños*

Smoked, or chipotle, chillies are very popular, and it is often high on the list of chilli growers to have a go at smoking as a means of preservation and for the unique flavour.

Chipotle is a word from the native Mexican language, Nahuatl, which literally means 'smoked chilli' though a chipotle to us is almost always a smoked Jalapeño chilli.

There are many ways of smoking chillies; the following list is just a few ways of doing it at home:

Cooker-top smoker: A simple metal container where the food to be smoked sits on a rack above some wood chips which smoulder slowly as they are cooked on the heat of the cooker ring below.

A purpose-built Hot Smoker, such as a Bradley Smoker®: These thermostatically control the heat and generate smoke from briquettes that sit on an electric element. These are expensive but effective.

The kettle BBQ method: Lay your chillies on the rack at one end of a lidded BBQ, put wood chips above some hot coals the other end, close the lid and wait.

None of these methods are designed specifically for chillies so there is always a degree of experimentation involved, but food smoking is a hobby in itself and really becomes quite addictive so there is always some fun to be had. It is unlikely that chillies (especially fleshy Jalapeños) will be fully dried by the smoking process so they will need to be fully dried by some other means afterwards.

Big Bombs sliced and ready for pickling

Pickling

The basic pickling mixture for chillies is 48% water, 48% vinegar, 2% salt and 2% sugar.

For small chillies pierce them or slice them open to let the mixture penetrate and stuff them into jars. Bigger chillies can be sliced or chopped.

Heat the liquid mixture to boiling point, let it cool slightly, pour it into the jars and seal the lids.

Steer clear of malt vinegar as it will stain the chillies and they will all end up dull brown. Use white wine, cider or rice wine vinegar.

This is the basic recipe which ensures they are preserved properly; you can make your own variations on this theme by using different vinegars, adding garlic, herbs, other vegetables or spices.

Chilli Oil

To make chilli oil you should only use dried chillies. It is a simple process; make holes in each chilli so the oil can get inside, stuff them into a bottle with an oil of your choice and leave to stand for a few weeks so the flavour infuses. Simple and tasty.

Putting fresh chillies in oil is not a way of preserving them. They will rot, as there is moisture trapped in the chilli which will still allow bacteria to grow and the danger is that Botulism will flourish. Botulism is an anaerobic bacterium (it lives without air) and so the fact that the chilli is 'sealed' by the oil isn't enough to stop it growing. If you do put fresh chillies in oil it will need to be refrigerated and only have a shelf life of a couple of weeks.

Hot Sauce

An obvious use of your chillies will be to try and make some hot sauce from them. The basic hot sauce recipe isn't far different from the pickling recipe, except the sauce is blended to make it smooth.

48% chillies, 50% vinegar, 2% salt. Boil all the ingredients together and use a food blender to get the right consistency before you bottle it. The purpose of the vinegar is to keep the pH (acidity) level high enough so that bacteria can't grow in the sauce, the salt helps with preservation too.

Like pickling, this is a base for experimentation; you can substitute some of the vinegar with fruit juice or add herbs and spices, there are many recipes available on the internet for you to try.

Other recipes have a high sugar content, which is another way of stopping harmful bacteria growing.

Be careful when trying to copy the ingredients of commercially produced sauces; although their vinegar content might be low they often have artificial preservatives to make up for the lack of vinegar. These may only be present in very small quantities, but they are crucial to keeping the sauce safe for consumption.

WHAT'S NEXT?

CHAPTER ELEVEN

What's Next?

More Difficult Varieties

As previously mentioned, there are some varieties notorious for their poor germination, slow growth rate or need for constant higher temperatures.

Jamaican Hot Chocolate

This is a Capsicum chinenese; a Habañero or Scotch Bonnet, depending on where you come from. It is sometimes difficult to germinate and is quite slow growing, but, if you can overcome those hurdles, then you could be rewarded with a huge bush bearing hundreds of chocolate coloured extremely hot and tasty chillies.

Jamaican Hot Chocolate

Trinidad Scorpion 'Butch T' – The title of 'Hottest Chilli' has changed a few times in the last couple of years, but, at the time of printing, this is the current record-holder. If you fancy something 200 times hotter than a Jalapeño then give this one a go.

Tepin **–** This sometimes has poor germination and, again, takes a long time to fruit. Also the yield is very low. However, if you are really interested in chillies then it might be worthwhile trying this one as it is a good example of what a wild chilli looks like, the type that our popular, modern varieties originated from. Of all varieties this is also the most tolerant of cold, so you might find it easier to over-winter. In fact it isn't really worth considering unless you intend to keep it for more than a year, as it is unlikely to fruit before the end of September in its first season.

Harvesting and Keeping Seeds

You may wish to keep the seeds from the chillies you have grown yourself or from some you have bought from a shop, and doing so is very easy, but there are a few things to bear in mind about growing from saved seeds.

Ideally, the chillies from which you take seeds should be undamaged, free of obvious disease and ripe to their final colour, but not to the point where they have started to soften. Seeds taken from green chillies probably won't have formed fully and will not germinate or will have a low germination rate.

Cut the chilli open, and carefully scrape out the seeds, discarding any that look blackened (except of course Rocoto Chillies whose seeds are characteristically black).

Lay them out on a piece of dry tissue or paper and leave them in a warm, dry place for a day or two until they have fully dried.

Put them in an airtight container such as a small jar or plastic zip-lock bag and label them. Store them in a cool, dry, dark place and they should be viable for at least a couple of years if not more.

Breeding and Cross-Pollination

There are a couple of things to bear in mind when saving seeds.

Firstly, beware that chilli plants cross-pollinate very easily and any plants grown close to each other may have been cross-pollinated by insects. This will not affect the fruit that develops on those plants, but any seeds saved from them might produce unexpected results when they, in turn, are planted and produce fruit.

This is a double-edged sword. If you want to grow exactly what you had this year then you will need to protect your plant from cross-pollination by shrouding it in netting, or keep it isolated in some way from other chilli plants.

Alternatively the fact that chillies cross so readily means you may get something completely different the following year and, if you cultivate that for a few generations to make sure it remains stable, then you have a new variety all of your own. For many people this is part of the fun but remember that it isn't all about the chilli itself, when selectively breeding chillies you may inadvertently lose some vital characteristics such as yield, disease resistance, growth rate, or compact foliage. To take full advantage of controlled breeding you would need to keep plants apart from others and selectively cross-pollinate by hand in order to avoid random results.

Another thing to remember is that some varieties such as Apache, Cheyenne or Cherry Bomb are what is known as 'F1'. This is a plant breeders' term used to describe something which is itself a direct descendant of two different parents and if you keep the seeds from these plants you may also get erratic results.

None of this should deter you from having a go at breeding new varieties yourself. In the past, domestic growers have managed to reach 'the holy grail' of chilli growing and produce plants that have been awarded the record for the hottest chilli in the world, potentially a very lucrative achievement. These varieties may not be stable through subsequent generations, it takes a few years of controlled breeding to achieve this, but you never know where your hobby will take you!

RESOURCES & INDEX

Resources

Nemaslug®, Aphidius and other biological controls

Green Gardener
Chandlers End, Mill Road, Stokesby, Gt Yarmouth NR29 3EY
01493 750061
www.greengardener.co.uk

Peat-Free Compost

Vital Earth GB Ltd
Blenheim Road, Airfield Industrial Estate, Ashbourne, Derbyshire DE6 1HA
0800 973555
www.thegreenergardener.com

Seeds

Remember there are plenty of seed sellers in the USA that will post seeds to the UK and Europe

Tomato Growers
www.tomatogrowers.com

South Devon Chilli Farm
Wigford Cross, Loddiswell, Kingsbridge, Devon TQ7 4DX
01548 550782
www.southdevonchillifarm.co.uk

Nicky's Nursery
01843 600972
www.nickys-nursery.co.uk

The Chilli Pepper Company
01539 558110
www.chilliseeds.co.uk

Seeds of Italy (Franchi Seeds)
www.seedsofitaly.com
or available from garden centres

Growing Kits

South Devon Chilli Farm
(see opposite column for contact details)

Smoking Equipment

Bradley Smoker UK
4 Halwell Business Park, Halwell, Totnes, Devon TQ9 7LQ
01803 712712
www.bradleysmoker.co.uk

Bradley Smoker USA / Canada
Bradley Technologies Canada Inc. 8380 River Road, Delta, BC, V4G 1B5
www.bradleysmoker.com

Hydroponics and Assisted Growing Systems

Greenhouse Sensation
Towngate Works, Mawdesley, L40 2QU
0845 6023774
+44(0) 1695 554097
www.greenhousesensation.co.uk

Index

Aji 9

Apache 15, 24, **27**, **29**, 95

Aphid

- *See also* Greenfly
- companion planting 68
- control **71-72**

Aphidius 72

Bacterial Spot 76

Bhut Jolokia 28

Biological Controls **67**, 75

Birdseye (chilli) 8, 60

Blackfly **71-72**, 75

Breeding (new varieties) 94

Capsaicin

- effect on mice 78
- effect on slugs 69
- growing conditions 60
- measurement 7

Capsicum annuum **9**, 27, 57, 61

Capsicum baccatum **9**, 13, 16, 28, 53

Capsicum chinense **9**, 13, 26, 28, 53, 58

Capsicum frutescens **8**, 28

Capsicum pubescens **10**

Caterpillars 73-74

Cayenne 9, **28**, 56, 61, 86

Cherry Bomb 95

Cheyenne 15, **27**, 29, 95

Chilli oil 88

Chiltepin 38

Chipotle 24,27

- home smoking 87

Corking (scarring of skin) 62

Damping-off (of seedlings) 37, 39, **46**

Drying chillies 86

F1 varieties 95

Feeding

- larger plants 52, **54**
- seedlings 45
- whilst fruiting 59

Fish Pepper 62

Flowers

- flower drop 58
- on poorly fed plants 56
- pollination **57**

Freezing (as means of preserving) 85

Fungus gnats 75

Germination **37-38**

- temperatures 14
- viability of seed 36

Ghost Chilli *see* Bhut Jolokia
Greenfly **71-72**
    also see Aphids
Greenhouse **15**
    beds 52
    growing conditions 13
    humidity 58
    plastic covered 16
Growing kits 39
Habañero **9**, **28-30**
    drying 86
    germination 38
    growing conditions 13
    heat 60
    over winter 81
    Hot Chocolate (chilli) 93
Hardening-Off 47
Heat (of fruit)
    measurement 7
    of varieties 27-28
Hoop Houses *see* Polytunnels
Hot sauce 89
Humidity
    flower drop 58
    pollination 57
    seedlings 39
Hungarian Wax 26, **27**
Hydroponics 17
Jalapeño 9, 25, **27**, 29
    blackening 61
    chipotle 24
    corking 62
    smoking 87
Jamaican Hot Chocolate 28, 93
    germination 38
    over winter 81
Joe's Long 28
LED (lighting) 19
Malagueta 8
Medusa **22**, 23, 34, 56
Mice 78
Mulato 38
Naga Jolokia *see* Bhut Jolokia
Nitrogen
    in plant feed 55
    results of high nitrogen feed 58
Nutrient Film Technique 19
NFT *see* Nutrient Film Technique
Orange Habañero *see* Habañero
Origins (of chillies) 7
Overwatering 68
Peat
    and the environment 4
Phosphorous 56
Phytophthora Blight 77
Picking 63
Pickling (chillies) 27, **88**
Pimiento de Padrón 26, **27**, 63
Poblano **27**, 30
    over winter 81
Pollination 57-59
Polytunnels 16
    and mice 78
Potassium 55
Pots
    for seedlings 43
    larger plants 51
    seeds 33-34
    self watering 19
Prairie Fire 23, **27**
Propagators 13, **35**
Pruning 55
    during winter 81
Purple Flash 62

Red Spider Mite 74-75, 77
Rocoto 10, 94
Scotch Bonnet **9**, 13, 28, 30, 93
also see Habañero
Scoville Scale 7
Serrano 27
blackening 61
corking 62
SHU *see* Scoville Scale
Slugs 69-71
biological control 67
Smoking Chillies 24, **87**
Snails 69-71
Species 8
Spelling 3
Sun damage
seedlings 45, **47**
Sunscald of fruit 77
Sweet peppers 9
blossom-end rot 76
over winter 81
Tabasco 8, 81
Tepin 38, 81, 94
Thai chillies 8, 23, 28-29
over winter 81
Tobacco Mosaic Virus 77
Transplanting 44
Trinidad Scorpion 28, 93
Twilight 27
Variegation 62
Vermiculite 33-34, 37
Verticillium Wilt 77
Watering
seedlings 45
seeds 37
plants 52
Whitefly 71, **73**

Acknowledgments

All photos by the author except:

Auto Watering System, NFT system (Chapter 3). Greenhouse Sensation

About the Author

Jason Nickels has been a chilli enthusiast since they were forced upon him in early childhood. In his younger days he made all the mistakes a novice grower is likely to make. Luckily he learned from these mistakes and extensive travel to South America in his 20s only served to enhance his knowledge and experience of chillies.
His hobby grew and in 2003 he was a founder of South Devon Chilli Farm, a commercial chilli grower and supplier of seeds and chilli plants to domestic growers in the U.K. He has made numerous TV appearances, written magazine features and delivered talks on chilli growing to enthusiastic audiences. His experience and knowledge of the challenges faced by novice and domestic chilli growers is unparalleled. Jason has now retired from commercial farming and lives in Devon with his wife Katrina.

Contact: growingchilliesbook@gmail.com

Lightning Source UK Ltd.
Milton Keynes UK
UKHW050436040321
379747UK00004B/101

* 9 7 8 0 9 5 7 4 4 4 6 0 7 *